Series 606F

S Sandra Atkinson Atkinson
3 374 Limesdale gdns Limesdale gdns
Edgware
Middx
265-0638 35 8
Edgware
Middx
class 2J
Room 12

'Through the Ages'
FOOD

by MURIEL GOAMAN

with illustrations by
FRANK HAMPSON

Publishers WILLS & HEPWORTH Ltd Loughborough
First published 1968   ©   *Printed in England*

To-day, you eat your dinner off a plate, using a knife and fork.

The first men who lived on the earth could not do this. They had no homes, but slept under trees or in caves. They did not wear clothes, and had only their long hair to keep them warm.

These people wandered about, eating wild berries and nuts. Sometimes they dug up roots to eat.

They caught small animals in the woods, and fish from the rivers.

7214 0090 6

Later, men began to make tools and weapons of stone. They found that sharp flints could be used to kill animals, and to cut them up.

Because of these stone weapons, we call this time the 'Stone Age'.

These people found that a fire could be started by rubbing two dry sticks together.

Now they could cook the animals they killed. The skins could be used for clothes.

Then they learned how to tame some of the wild animals. Cows and goats gave milk. Dogs and horses were useful for hunting.

Sometimes, seeds and berries used for food fell onto the ground. The seeds grew up into new, young plants.

Then, perhaps, men had the idea of planting seeds themselves. They may have stirred the earth with a stick. This would have made the plants grow bigger.

The first hoe could have been a deer's horn tied to a branch.

Slowly, men learned to farm. They tried out different sorts of crops.

When there was plenty of food for all, the people lived together in small villages.

How did these early people learn to make bread?

Perhaps they found some seeds too hard to crack between their teeth. So they tried to crush the seeds between two smooth stones.

Some of the seeds may have been wheat. Perhaps water was added to the crushed wheat, making a thick paste.

Some of the paste was cooked in clay pots. Some was formed into little cakes, and cooked over hot ashes.

It was the first bread, but not at all like the bread we eat to-day.

After thousands of years, the Stone Age was slowly followed by the Bronze Age, when men learned to make tools and weapons from a metal called bronze.

This Age was slowly followed by the Iron Age, when even stronger tools, and even ploughs, were made from iron.

The Iron Age people were defeated when Roman armies, from Italy, invaded Britain in 43 A.D.

The Romans then ruled Britain. They built themselves better houses than the Britons had seen before. Every house had a kitchen, with a brick and stone hearth for cooking.

After about four hundred years the Romans left Britain. Fierce raiders came over from the German forests.

Many Roman towns were burnt and destroyed. The invaders lived in bare, wood and stone huts. These stood in villages, with big fields around.

There were no kitchens. The man in the picture is shown roasting meat on an iron spit. He turned the spit around to cook the meat evenly on each side.

When the meat was cooked, it was eaten straight off the spit.

These people were called Anglo-Saxons.

The Anglo-Saxons used oxen to draw the plough. Two important crops were grown in the fields.

One was wheat to make bread. The other was barley to make beer. Honey was used to make a sweet drink called mead.

Sheep and pigs lived on the waste land outside the village. They were used for meat. The wool of the sheep was used for clothes.

The Anglo-Saxons did not have much better food than the early Britons.

Sugar was unknown in those days. Honey had been used for many years. This was found in the nests of wild bees in trees or decayed logs. It was difficult to collect.

People began to keep their own bees. Straw was twisted into tall, round hives for the bees. These were called 'skeps'.

When the honey was ready to be taken, the bees had to be killed. If they were not killed, the bees would have stung anyone who came near the skep.

This was a great waste of bees.

In the Norman period (the twelfth century) meals became much richer.

The great hall of the manor house was used for eating. The kitchen was a long way from the hall. In winter, food must have been almost cold by the time it reached the table.

Daggers were used to carve the meat off huge joints. People plunged their hands into the main dish. Hunks of bread were used to mop up the gravy.

Every manor house had an orchard Apples, pears, plums and cherries were grown.

Sugar was first brought to England from Venice in Henry III's reign (the thirteenth century).

It was coloured pink and violet. For many years it was looked upon as a rare spice. People went on using honey for sweetening.

After America was discovered, sugar became much cheaper in England. Sugar-cane grows in America.

Hundreds of years later, it was found that sugar could be got from sugar-beet. This grows in Britain. By 1920, large crops of sugar-beet were growing in this country.

To-day, we use cane and beet sugar for sweetening.

In early days, salt was hard to get. It was very dear, and few people could afford it.

Rich people used salt to preserve meat for the winter. Poor people went hungry in cold weather.

In wealthy families, salt was put on the table for the important guests only. It was placed in a 'salt-foot'. We would call this our salt-cellar.

The salt-foot stood half-way down the table. The rich and people of high rank sat 'above the salt'. The poor people and servants sat 'below the salt'.

There was no food for the animals during the winter. Each year, many sheep and oxen were killed off before the cold weather began.

The lord of the manor had plenty of deer, rabbits and birds in his woods. He could catch fish in his rivers.

The poor, hungry peasants used to 'poach' or steal these.

Strict laws were passed in the fourteenth century to stop this poaching. They were called 'Game-Laws'.

Game keepers hid in the woods to catch poachers. If they were caught, they were punished very severely.

The fifteenth century housewife could not just run down to the shops, as mothers do to-day. Only the big towns had shops.

Many things could not be grown or made in England. Wine came from France. Spices came from the Far East. They were needed to hide the taste of the salted meat which did not keep well.

The lady of the manor had to plan far ahead. Every summer she filled huge store-rooms with all sorts of foods, preserved for the winter.

Would you like to eat all your meals without any potatoes?

They have been known in England for only four hundred years.

In the reign of Queen Elizabeth the First, many brave men sailed to the New World (which we know as America). These sailors must have seen their first potatoes there.

Some say that Sir Walter Raleigh first brought potatoes to England. Others think it was Captain John Hawkins, who lived at the same time.

At first, British people did not like potatoes, and would not eat them.

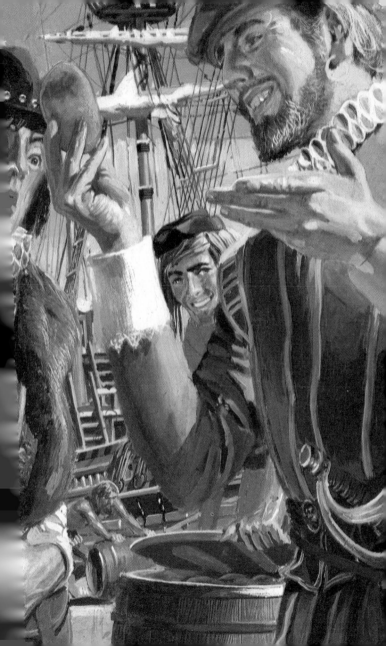

For hundreds of years, spits were used for roasting meat. The spit turned a joint around in front of a roaring fire. The fat from the meat fell into a dish on the floor. This fat became what we call 'dripping'.

Sometimes, a kitchen-boy turned the handle of the spit. During the seventeenth century, dogs were used.

The dog was put inside a big wheel, hanging on the wall. As the dog walked along, the wheel turned. This worked the spit.

Later, clock-work spits were invented.

For many hundreds of years, people ate food just because they were hungry. They did not ask if the food was good for them.

Sometimes, they could eat fruit and fresh meat. At other times, both were scarce.

Sailors in the Navy ran short of some foods on long voyages. After many weeks on board, the men became ill.

In 1772, Captain Cook had the idea that his men needed fresh fruit. A rule was made that they must all have lemons every day.

This ended an illness called 'scurvy'.

From very early days, wheat has been ground to make flour. At first, this was done by hand.

After man found how to make a wheel, he built a mill. The mill ground wheat between two stones.

Sometimes, mill stones were turned by a water-wheel. Later, mills were built with huge sails. The wind turned the sails.

Windmills are beautiful. You can still see them sometimes in the countryside.

In 1879, mills worked by machines were built in England. These mills grind wheat into very fine flour.

Coffee was brought to England first in 1600. For more than two hundred years only a few people could afford to drink it.

Tea soon followed coffee. It was called 'tay'. In 1651, tea cost ten pounds a pound. That was a large sum in those days. A 'dish of tea', as it was called, was a sign of wealth.

The wise housewife kept her tea locked away.

In 1828, tea was found growing wild in India. Tea plantations were started. Tea became much cheaper.